TO IRELAND, WITH LOVE

ALICE BOYD STOCKDALE

TO IRELAND, WITH LOVE

1964
DOUBLEDAY & COMPANY, INC.
GARDEN CITY, NEW YORK

Thanks are due to the following periodicals in whose pages some of these poems have appeared: *The Saturday Evening Post*, "Thoughts While Climbing Howth Hill" © 1957 The Curtis Publishing Company (appeared under the title "First Spring"); *The Diplomat*, "Calling Card"; *Ladies' Home Journal*, "Winter Night" © 1960 The Curtis Publishing Company; Dublin *Sunday Independent*, "In Memory of Scott McLeod" and "Solitude in Enniskillen"; University of Miami *Poetry Chapbook*, "Eivlin, Eivlin" (appeared under the title "Daughter, Daughter"); *The Irish Press*, "Sunday Suppers"; Dublin *Opinion*, "On Taking a Painting to 20 Molesworth Street," "Tea," and "Help!" (appeared under the title of "American Tourist"); *The Tablet*, London, "Coastal Wives"; *The Kerryman*, "The Orphans' Band in Tralee"; *Kilkenny People*, "Letter of Protest"; *McCall's*, "Magpies" and "The Children's Hour."

Ireland has a way of casting its spell over all who go to live there. One lady who fell in love with Ireland is Alice Boyd Stockdale, wife of the United States Ambassador to Ireland in 1961–62. Entranced with the country, she put her wonder into rhyme, and the result is this book, *To Ireland, with Love.*

Mrs. Stockdale has a keen eye, a gift for rhymes, and a sensitivity to the beauty of both nature and people. There are some fine and fresh impressions of Ireland in this book. The author pokes around the antique shops and bookstores of Dublin, goes out to Wexford Harbour, and Ballynahinch. We can share her own enchantment with emerald beauty of the countryside.

Alice Boyd Stockdale also has a sensitivity to life and history. To her, life is rich and exciting enough to be worthy of the effort of a poem. She shares with us such varied experiences as finding a pheasant hanging in the larder of an old kitchen, watching American Westerns on Irish television, and preparing for diplomatic receptions. She catches the irony of a rich man's daughter, during the Great Famine, being reassured that all is well, despite the suffering she sees.

For those who have themselves fallen in love with Ireland, these poems will stir happy memories. For those who have never been there, it will serve to whet the appetite. Mrs. Stockdale had a unique opportunity, as an ambassador's wife, to sample every section and every level of life in Ireland. We are richer for her having been there.

EDWARD M. KENNEDY
United States Senate

For Grant with whom, hand in hand,
I walked through Phoenix Park . . .
and who will always walk with me.

CONTENTS

I. IN DUBLIN

THOUGHTS WHILE CLIMBING HOWTH HILL

AT A BOOKSTALL ON NASSAU STREET

FITZWILLIAM SQUARE

O'CONNELL STREET AFTER RAIN

CITYSCAPE

ON TAKING A PAINTING TO 20 MOLESWORTH STREET

RAINY AFTERNOONS

ON READING DUBLIN'S SIX NEWSPAPERS

SECOND MEETING

THOUGHTS ON EDMUND BURKE

ON THE OUTSKIRTS OF DUBLIN

DESCENT INTO DUBLIN

THOUGHTS WHILE
CLIMBING HOWTH HILL

I think that God
tossed into spring
a large handful of birds
to sing
as He Himself
grew lyrical
witnessing
His miracle.

AT A BOOKSTALL ON NASSAU STREET

Dawdling his fingers
in the Fountain of Pirene,
the old professor lingers
at a table in the rain.

Although bifocals long have blurred
Helicon and mane,
beneath the awning the absurd
chimera, Time, lies slain.

FITZWILLIAM SQUARE

The prim old Georgian houses sit
Implacably in rows,
Each aching more than she'll admit,
Each looking down her nose
And holding fast a fluted fan
To elegant façade,
A noble and rheumatic clan
Defying man and God.

O'CONNELL STREET AFTER RAIN

Sun shafts, after rain, ensnare
each floating particle in air;
Dublin shimmers golden-pale
like a city under sail,
gliding imperceptibly
from the mountains toward the sea.

Grass in Stephen's Green is glittering,
spinnaker clouds softly skittering
over Grafton Street and gilding
Trinity's gate and limestone building;
lustrous Oliver Goldsmith stands
dripping bronze from both his hands.

The anchor of the bridge is lifting,
cargo casually shifting
as the city seems to slip
through tawny vapour like a ship
with Nelson's Pillar for the tallmast,
black O'Connell Street for ballast.

CITYSCAPE

If I could settle down on Usher's Quay
Halfway between the Brewery and O'Connell,
Setting an easel up in front of me
Beside the doorway of Draper's, O'Donnell,
I'd take to brush and palette and I'd shape
The afternoon into a cityscape.

First, I'd lightly pencil in the Liffey
Slanting up the canvas left to right
(The sunny sky should be salt water taffy
With several flapping seagulls caught in flight.)
And sketching Arran Quay, I'd string its little
Row of buildings right across the middle.

I've never had a painting brush in hand,
So naturally would be disposed to fumble
As I mixed lavenders and mauves, and planned
Just how to stay a horse and wagon's rumble.
I'd feel quite like an artist in Montmartre,
The Court of Justice being Sacred Heart. . . .

The technique being rather like Utrillo,
The river reflecting dashes of Monet;
Perhaps the swans would slightly list, but still, oh,
I'd never give my afternoon away.
I'd take it down to Dawson Street and frame it,
"On Usher's Quay" is what I'd simply name it.

ON TAKING A PAINTING
TO 20 MOLESWORTH STREET

Since it's small enough to carry,
I came running, Mr. Gorry;
even though it's dark and blurry
I am hoping you can *hurry*,
for the dealer told the story
it's a *Lely*, and I'm wary
though we'd surely not be sorry
if we found, in all the flurry,
it's a *Jervas*, Mr. Gorry!

You say I needn't worry?
There isn't any hurry?
It's signed a Mr. Murray?
WHO'S HE?

RAINY AFTERNOONS

It seems the law of averages
on rainy afternoons
that I retreat to Savage's
to poke among the spoons.
A cat is dozing on the sill
amid old jewels and medals,
and steaming tea attacks the chill
that films the copper kettles.

The floor is slanted, but toes-in,
and stepping single file,
two customers, with elbows in,
can make a little aisle
and touch a century or so
on either silver side
here in Georgian Dublin
ten feet wide;

Then up the narrow winding stairs,
another musty storey, a
treasure-trove of china, chairs
and phantasmagoria,
with tables wobbly on their legs
and oil lamps meant to tease one,
all boldly marked with tiny tags
expressly writ to please one.

To Savage's, to Savage's
I'd rather go than eat,
and while away a rainy day
on Lower Liffey Street.

ON READING DUBLIN'S
SIX NEWSPAPERS

When Mercury's talaria,
of ancient myth, collided
violently with flying cranes,
the startled flock divided,
white plumes erupting into chains
of symbols, broken-sided. . . .

through sunny and celestial lanes
the letters formed and glided
as alphabet; their heart's-desire land
lay below them . . . fertile Ireland!
Here, daily evidence remains,
the printed word resided.

SECOND MEETING

(with a literary critic)

I'll meet you at the Shelbourne
this afternoon for tea
and we'll take up where we left off
discussing poetry,
and you'll repeat that it is *dead*
and I will disagree.

We'll settle by a window
overlooking Stephen's Green,
you and I (with Mr. Yeats
sandwiched in between)
and watch the cadence of the crowd
upon the lyric scene.

I'll pour a cup for Whitman
and you'll stir a cup for Joyce;
to Mr. Yeats we'll offer up
the biscuit of his choice,
and nibble quite contentedly
above the smoke and noise.

Then you will *crash* your teacup down
and Mr. Yeats will flee,
beckoning to Dickinson
and Frost and Gogarty,
while you interpret bitter dregs
as future poetry.

We'll cavil, disagreeing friends,
in words as sharp as alum
and then at the revolving doors
you'll leave the Shelbourne, solemn,
as I greet Thomas Kinsella
and nod to Padraic Colum.

THOUGHTS ON EDMUND BURKE
(1729–97)
WHILE LUNCHING AT THE BAILEY

The Bailey's much the same old pub
with pleasant smell of hops and dampness,
same floorboard squeaks beneath hubbub
of casual Trinity students, I guess,
as when young Burke dropped in from class,
dumped books and called for a glass of ale,
  "On the whole, the qualities of beauty,
  as they are merely sensible qualities,
  are the following: First to be
  comparatively small.
and took the first long draught,
  "Secondly, to be smooth.
inspecting the minute bubbles polliwogging
toward the foam
  "Thirdly, to have a variety in the direction
  of the parts;
and dispersing,
  "but Fourthly, to have those parts not
  angular, but melted as it were into each other.
then turning the glass slowly around
  "Fifthly, to be of a delicate frame,
  without any remarkable appearance of strength.
and holding it to the light
  "Sixthly, to have its colour clear and bright,
  but not very strong and glaring.
before one last swallow,
  "These are, I believe, the properties on which
  beauty depends; properties that operate by
  nature, and are less liable to be altered by
  caprice, or confounded by a diversity of tastes,
  *than any other."**
finally collecting his books, tossing a penny on the table
and entering the rain.

* Part III, Section XVIII, *On The Sublime and Beautiful*, Edmund Burke

ON THE OUTSKIRTS
OF DUBLIN

The herd-boy ambling on before us
parts the cattle with his stick.
Ho! he cries, his cold breath rising
from the sudden exercising.
Car creeps, easing through the thick
herd protesting in a chorus.

Bobbing heads with brown-eyed stares
press about the window glass;
lumbering steers close ranks behind us
loudly clanging to remind us
as they, grudging, let us pass
that this suburban road is theirs.

DESCENT INTO DUBLIN

The sky is rounding like a cup
as white horizon straightens up;
it's good to see the place you know
appearing through the clouds below,
to see the misty city rise
and greet you swooping from the skies.
  Bay, once curving line,
  is fluted valentine
  where deep and shallow shade
  into blue brocade.
  Howth Hill I climbed one day
  is detail in the Bay,
  busy roads I travelled,
  balls of yarn unravelled;
  precisely, Phoenix Park
  is squared with all its dark
  lanes becoming one
  emerald in the sun—
  St. Mary's, and our tall house
  sitting like a dollhouse;
  the Liffey spins a thread
  of silk from overhead
  and downtown, cuts through olden
  buildings crowded golden;
  far as sharp eye wills
  the boa of the hills
  curls a purple arm
  around the blur of farm;
then suddenly the streets have people,
every church is topped with steeple,
cars have wheels; houses, windows,
runway that was long and thin goes
hard and wide beneath the plane.
The engines off, I'm home again.

II. AT HOME IN PHOENIX PARK

IN MEMORY OF SCOTT McLEOD

(Former U. S. Ambassador to Ireland)
November 1961

Today I walk around the grounds,
Nothing here escapes the news;
November breaks with mournful sound
Beneath my shoes.

A dove is throbbing overhead,
The orchard droops with bitter fruit,
And over all, the lowered flag
is hanging mute.

Dublin's hills lie brooding now;
an ancient bell intones a hymn
Across the Park where even cow
Stands cold of limb.

Beloved acres! Now he owns you,
Meadow, wall and tall trees leaning;
Evermore he strolls your lawns
To watch them greening.

ON FINDING A PHEASANT
HANGING IN THE LARDER

Pheasant, it was not enough
That you couched, November-brown,
Where a cold and purple thicket
Hid your purple crown.

Scarlet berry, groundsel leaf,
Copper gall, mushroom cluster
Camouflaged your silk, yet failed
To cache your lustre.

Sunlight caught your iridescence,
Huntsman halted, squinting eye,
Pheasant . . . winter stabs me
Seeing color die.

PORTRAIT OF BRIDGET
SHELLING PEAS

Kitchen-bound, she is led
Down country byways when she settles
In a sunny chair and spreads
Her apron out, with peas and kettles.

These come, she knows not from what patch,
From whose straw hamper overflowing;
She only knows that she can catch
The scent of County Wexford growing,

And thoughts turn fresh as furrowed sod
Yielding with the sudden snap
Of summer bursting from a pod,
Of childhood falling in her lap.

MAGPIES

The clowns of birddom
waddle and chatter,
discussing a most
important matter

concerning crumbs—
then clear their throats
and leave tongue-twisting
thank-you notes.

FEBRUARY WALK

When chimneys blow with burning wood
and meadows smell of smouldering scutch
beneath a rake, and turning sod
reveals a crowded rabbit hutch,

when sweetness from the butterburs
assails the path and finds the rare
and fragrant tang of flowering furze;
when cold sun filters through the air

and resin breath drifts from the pines;
when partridges survey the glen,
nose-deep, slow cattle munch designs
in fields of clover once again.

SUMMER SUNDAY
IN PHOENIX PARK

Seventeen hundred and sixty acres wide,
the Park is luring Dubliners outside,
suggesting slow safaris through the Zoo
and rows of benches on the Avenue.

Young riders from Park Gate come clopping in
to watch bicycle races that begin
near the U. S. Ambassador's residence;
passers-by are leaning on a fence

admiring the formal gardens and the lawn
of their stately Aras an Uachtarain
while harriers puff past with elbows up.
Beyond the trees a languid kite goes up

and over by the Papal Nuncio's,
tableclothes are spread while fathers doze
oblivious to children and the snatches
of far-off cheers that rise from rugby matches.

Down toward Castleknock beside the Gate
the timid deer and cattle congregate
to stare at cars that finally trickle by
as Northern Lights invade the summer sky.

Ten-thirty now, and in this green oasis
the timpani of cricket song displaces
Sunday laughter; dark discreetly hovers
like a blanket over lingering lovers.

TWILIGHT RENDEZVOUS

At twilight, the accustomed hour,
the courtly deer, en masse,
traverse the Park . . . the cows bestir
to let them gently pass
and always a protective gull
escorts them to the house.

Gingerly we take the lawn
to watch them feed and huddle:
the velvet does and spotted fawns
beyond the ha-ha, idle,
and antlered stags that disregard
the cowbells' golden rattle.

As in museums, they turn and stare,
frozen motionless;
we dare not breathe or move a hair
or let a leaf fall lest
the deer, with curious heartbeat
triggered, disappear.

YOUNG MAN, STROLLING

Young man, I have seen you strolling
In the silence of the Park
Day after day, hand in pocket
Of the slim, familiar jacket,
Twilight into dark.

I have come to know your whistle,
Know your collie, know your cap;
Have seen the straggling sunlight hold you,
Watched the emerald grass enfold you
In its loving lap.

With your lichened switch I see you
Flick the mushrooms in your way,
And I know what you are thinking.
Would that, through the soft mist falling,
You could hear a stranger calling:
Stay.

III. ON THE OFFICIAL SIDE

CALLING CARD

GUEST BOOK

TRIOLET

ARRANGING FLOWERS

DIPLOMATIC IMMUNITY

TEA

DIPLOMATIC DINNER

CALLING CARD

O I will take it very hard
If ever dies the calling card,
    the calling card,
    the calling card
    I cannot do without.

I'm socially snug, officially saved
With tiny white ego, script-engraved.
    So strip from my wallet
    License to drive,
    Blood whatchacallit
    To keep me alive,
    Internal Revenue receipt,
Leave my calling card fresh and neat.

    Take charge-a-plate
    And calorie chart
    And secret address
    Of a wholesale mart;
    Take photos, cash,
    Take all I own
But leave my calling card alone:

    It comforts me.
    I'll never lose it,
    And someday I may
    Even use it.

GUEST BOOK

It's rather a messed book
but still, it's our best book
which starts out normally,
names written formally
with neat addresses,
and then it progresses
to party guests, hurried,
who couldn't be worried
by crossing their t's;
then after these,
the signatures sprawled
by the famous who called
and suffered a sinking
spell during the inking
are mixed with our visitors,
lively inquisitors
whose American scratching
no doubt was catching.
A ponderous sheaf,
we treasure each leaf,
we'll pack it and date it
and someday translate it.

TRIOLET

The staff is in the staff room
while the telephone is ringing.
It's their radio and laugh room:
the staff is in the staff room,
a lively half-and-half room,
half jigging, and half singing.
The staff is in the staff room
while the telephone is ringing.

ARRANGING FLOWERS

Six vases for the drawing room,
three huge ones for the hall,
a bower for the ballroom
and ferny ones that sprawl
daintily for powder room;
a bold one for the cloakroom
and even an umbrella stand
explosive for the oak room;
copper bowls and silver bowls
as fast as I am able
for dining room and everywhere
except the billiard table.
I'm running out of vases,
I'm running out of hours,
I'm running out of places
and greenery and flowers—
to go beside the guest book
one last lotus,
probably the only one
anyone will notice.

DIPLOMATIC IMMUNITY

This spring the community
Sniffles and sneezes;
We'll see if Immunity
Covers diseases.

TEA

Tea in a cottage,
Tea in a manse,
Tea under Irish
Circumstance:

strong enough to trot a dog on,
hot enough to skin a rabbit,
black enough to float a bog on,
good enough to be a habit.

Tea in the States
Is often dodged
Because the taste
Is camouflaged:

sweetening enough to overpower,
ice enough to make it frosty,
lemon enough to turn it sour. . . .

No wonder American tea is nawsty.

DIPLOMATIC DINNER

Señor a la izquierda
Et Monsieur au droit,
Ne parlez pas,
Je vous en prie,
Ne parlez français over me,
The room's becoming hot.
My French is all forgot.

I smile and sip *Château Climens*
And fiddle with *Pâté foie gras,*
Embracing like a child
Le mot que je comprends.

It isn't very likely
That my charming *bon vivants*
Will interrupt their conversation,
Asking for my recitation
Of the poem of Ronsard's
Learned in college days which starts:
"Quand vous serai bien vieille . . ."

Through swimming candlelight I hear
The lilting laughter of the group
Down at the other end:
I even hear a friend
Whose English rises sweet and clear.

Alas, I'm not *très gai*
With no one sitting near to clue me,
Français swirling *par-dessus* me,
Château Climens not getting to me.

I smile and sip my soup.

IV. ALL IN THE FAMILY

FIRST SUNDAY IN CASTLEKNOCK CHURCH

SUNDAY SUPPERS

SUSAN AND PONY

FIRST IMPRESSIONS

WATCHING (AMERICAN) TV IN IRELAND

WINTER NIGHT

FAMILY PORTRAIT

FIRST SUNDAY
IN CASTLEKNOCK CHURCH

(St. Brigid's)

The girls from Mercer's School
all smile and nod,
and light flows multi-paned
upon the altar,
Now . . . *Behold the Body
and the Blood . . .*
the Chalice and the Host
are raised. I falter. . . .
Lord, You are the same,
we are Your flock,
and suddenly we're at home
in Castleknock.

SUNDAY SUPPERS

The family sups on Sunday night
According to its appetite,
Laying out the kitchen's hoard
For a stand-up smorgasbord.

While some prefer to simply munch
The cold remains of Sunday lunch,
Others carry steaming trays
Back to television plays.

Although the custom was designed
With weekend-weary Cook in mind,
She finds, when dishes all are stacked,
We banqueted instead of snacked.

SUSAN AND PONY

A patch of blue,
a patch of green,
a pasture, sunshine-gilt . . .
someday this day
will cover you
lightly as a quilt.
Some curious moment
out of time,
soft-scented as sachet:
a snatch of air,
a bit of brogue,
a flash of jackdaw jet,
a flap of flag,
a scrap of stile,
a flying mane will let
April come running
breathlessly,
scarf trailing,
sheer and gay,
sprinkling Ireland
over you,
bringing back
today.

FIRST IMPRESSIONS

MOUNTING ANXIETY

Now that I'm up as an equestrian,
Put me down as a pedestrian.

HELP!

I know 2/6
is thirty-five cents
but I can't seem to fix
in my mind if a pence
is more than a penny
or less, if any.

A pound is two eighty
but what is a bunny?
At last, I'm beginning
to learn Irish money.
Half-crowns are weighty,
here, let me show you . . .
*and please, while you're looking,
take out what I owe you.*

FINIS RAINBOW

We've studied the map
and found, to our horra,
there's no such place
as Glocca Morra.

WATCHING (AMERICAN) TV IN IRELAND

HIT THE TRAIL, COWBOY!

Buffaloes roam the Kerry Ring,
Arrows are flying in Clare;
Coyote song, it howls through Cong
And pintos are prowling Kildare.

O! Get ye back to Wy-o-ming,
Back to the lone prair-ie
Where never is heard a discouraging word,
Well anyway, not from me.

SHOOT 'EM UPS

I fear that some
escaping man'll
shoot me dead
right through the channel.

THE CHILDREN'S HOUR

Let's go upstairs and read Winnie the Pooh
After the murder on Channel 2.

MUSICAL SCORE

The Irish extol
Rock 'n' roll
On TV.

And who cares
For Irish airs?
Me.

WINTER NIGHT

Still she covers me
on a winter night,
fluffing out the comforter
of eider-down . . .
in the dark
her step is velvet;
flannel-soft,
her white nightgown.
I sense her warmth
and hear her slide
the window shut
as the wan street-light
catches
in the brown cascade
of hair hung loosely
down her back . . .
hair that turned to snow
before she died.

The room goes black.

Shivering,
I sit upright.
I'd better check the children.
It's cold tonight.

FAMILY PORTRAIT

Wind may shift,
buttercups go erratic,
let this shutter-click of time
preserve, emphatic,
quicksilver caught in color
on the lawn.

Let the Ambassador go on
relaxing with his left hand
on his knee, me perching
ever lightly at his shoulder
and Susan, like a captive leprechaun,
sagging, shy and smiling, in his arm.

Let motion unexpectedly collect
and Lee, insistent as a green tie,
stay a moment nine years old
and combed; let Ann alight an instant,
Thespis-winged, before resuming sky
and leaving Grant, upstanding as a prince.

May Sally poise, forever twenty-one,
and Ireland softly glint upon us all
before this curtain-drop
of handsome house while family,
split-seconded to fact,
remains intact.

V. PEOPLE

HARVEST

CONVERSATION AT ROUNDWOOD

GIRL IN DONEGAL

ON GWEEBARRA BAY

DUBLIN CHARACTER

THE OLD GARDENER

POOR TOM O'TOOLE

BIG JOHN

SANDYCOVE VIGNETTE

EMIGRANT

HARVEST

A friend of my Father
since Time began,
Mr. Neely was rather
a curious man:
when I was little
he'd come to call
and I'd perch in the middle
enchanted by all
the tingling towns
that tripped from his tongue,
lilting sounds
that to me, so young,
became a far-off
and misty island
where names like *Glengarriff*
were sweetly violined,
where *Skibbereen*
and *Inishvale*
tangled green
in a fairy tale.

I'd wait for his eyes
to brim with *Galway*,
a puzzling surprise
that happened always:
onto his vest
the tears would roll
and he'd try his best
to blow control
and go on with the story.
Bless his soul,
he's gone to glory
and never knew
that the seeds he'd sown
blossomed to fruit
when the child was grown.

CONVERSATION AT ROUNDWOOD

The older man, with arm around the younger,
(eighty years and eight, to be exact)
was bringing a narrative of Irish history
into the chair, more quickening than fact.
"And tell me, sir," the voice piped shy and thin,
"how many prisons were you *really* in?"

"Seven in Ireland, seven more in Britain,"
the accent dropped to confidential tone.
"*No!*" sighed the younger; "*Yes!*" replied the older. . . .
Faces close, the world became their own;
the Troubled Times were now, this very minute,
Past and Present merged and they were in it.

"And just how many years was that in all?"
"Let's see now, I would say six and a half."
"*No!*" sighed the younger; "*Yes!*" replied the older;
every now and then the two would laugh.
When Seán T. O'Kelly and Lee Stockdale parted,
sure, one was wiser, one was lighter-hearted.

GIRL IN DONEGAL

I'll not do it, Mother dear!
Look how the twilight lingers
and I'll not spend it sittin' here,
a needle in my fingers.

The sun is spreadin' on the rocks
and so I'll not be troublin'
my head about the fancy shops
that buy crochet in Dublin.

Curlews are cryin' on the shore,
my heart is cryin' too,
and I'll not spend a minute more
beside the hearth with you.

My neck, it grieves; my eyes, they twitch,
the sea is full of sky,
and I'll not take another stitch
of thread *tonight*. Goodbye!

ON GWEEBARRA BAY

Blow through me, wind!
Through heart . . . through
hair! Snatch from me each thought
of care. Whip me
as you whip my skirts
till all my little sins
and hurts careen like gulls
in random flight across the waters
out of sight.
All the loose bits of me, strip
like barnacles from off a ship.

Make of me
who has been closed,
an open *moonrise,*
bare, exposed. Make me one
with *channeled whelk,*
honed, submissive, smooth
as silk . . . then gently
as a glistening child who stumbles
on a shell, beguiled,
lift me, wind, unto your ear . . .
hold me fast
until you hear the singing
of my inner soul . . . now
let me down, refreshed
and whole.

DUBLIN CHARACTER

Agnes's cart's a cornucopia
of pears hand-polished, one by one;
of oranges gold as California,
apples big as Oregon.

Agnes and her fruit, I swear,
were conjured up by a magician.
At every race track, from thin air,
appears the toothless apparition.

At Leopardstown her hair is thatch,
her sweater bags at Baldoyle's meeting,
at Naas her pockets sag with cash;
she shrieks a Damon Runyon greeting

as soon as we step from the auto
at the Curragh or the Park,
her shrill and cackling vibrato
offering, each time, to mark

our card with winners, all for free,
and plying us with mammoth peaches.
"Anybody ask for me
back in America?" she screeches.

THE OLD GARDENER

Like agéd Renoir sculpting from his bed,
Paddy O'Rourke no longer pulls the weeds
Or wields a hoe; the younger men, instead,
Consider him the Master of the Seeds.

Paddy can tell the leafy from the rangy,
Which one lifts lavender and which one blue,
Just by putting his fingers in his pocket
And letting the little grains go dribbling through.

Inside his head he keeps a secret sundial
That measures time and sun by Irish laws,
And shuffling down a cinder path he reckons
That *here* is where Joe's barrow ought to pause.

In afternoons he sheds his coat and potters
Beneath the humid glass with bulbs and string
At table-height, where he can feel cool water's
Impact like the miracle of spring.

When twilight falls and Paddy strolls his garden,
He stands as does an artist from the frame,
Inspecting his design, and in soft brogue
He calls each flower by its Latin name.

POOR TOM O'TOOLE

Now, Tom O'Toole, you'd call as a rule,
an educated foreman,
but you'd never believe how the bloody fool
argued with us that mornin'.

Up we come cyclin' with shovel and pick
to continue working the highway,
and O'Toole, he starts to show us his charts
and he says, "Now we're doin' it *my* way!

"We're goin' to take *this*," he says with an air,
and he points to some city machinery,
"and like it or not, we're puttin' it *there!*"
And he points to a hill in the scenery.

"Oh no," says we, throwin' caps on the ground,
"you'll never get us to do it,
for everyone knows that's a *fairy mound*,
and we'd not put a bulldozer to it!"

What ejit, now, would go stirrin' up fairies?
We argued and idled and found it
was nearly a week till O'Toole, he shrieks,
"All right then, we'll go *around* it!"

Well, wouldn't you know that a Boston paper
carried the whole crazy mess,
so happy were they that the fairies still caper
up on the hill, I guess.

Poor Tom O'Toole was mentioned by name
and all of us laughed and laughed,
for while the fairies cavort the same,
Boston must think him daft!

BIG JOHN

Big John McDonald is an Irish giant
With boots all out of size and face of shale;
His gait's deliberate like a man who's spent
A lifetime leaning hard against a gale,
A man whose fingers grew to fit the boulders
He's jostled from the earth onto his shoulders.

Excitement in Mayo where he grew up
Was seeing signs of green along the furrows
Or slogging down a Dooleeg lane to sup
Or carting cabbage crops to town in barrows.
The wind and rain still lash his curious brogue
And Gaelic tangles in his dialogue.

The old cow-catcher rumbles day and night
In Dublin at the gate-house where he lives
Astride the driveway queerly, left and right,
In two small buildings . . . but the rumbling gives
Fine pleasure on a foggy night, in knowing
Just who it is that's coming in or going.

There's not an inch on all the sixty acres
That Big John doesn't know; why, he can tell
By looking at the firewood in the lockers
Which tree it's from and in what storm it fell;
His life's all out of doors in any weather,
Making watery eyes and hands of leather.

But oh, how gently on a snowy night,
His hands receive new lambs and set them going
Each side the heaving ewe in lantern light
That quivers like the mouths where life is flowing,
And for a third lamb coming, frail, unsteady,
The nursing bottle and Big John are ready.

SANDYCOVE VIGNETTE

(County Dublin, June 1904)

CHARACTERS:
Charwoman
Oliver St. John Gogarty
James Joyce

Bein' a charwoman, gettin' up at dawn,
you never know who you'll be comin' upon

staggerin' drunk at the divil's own hour.
Take this mornin' by the Martello Tower;

the sun was up and the sea all shiny
from clear up at Howth right on to Killiney,

and here they come, 'most fallin' down
from bein' all night on the town.

And young they were, and blue of eye,
and one was wavin' at the sky

a-shoutin'; far as I could see
his fancy words was Greek to me;

the other, a tenor clear as glass,
the kind you'd hear in a Sunday Mass,

was singin' like this: We-e-ep no mo-r-re!
Like now, I was sayin' before,

you never know who, so I stepped aside
and dead in their tracks they give me a wide

sweep of their hats and a grandee bow,
and keepin' their balance, don't ask me how,

the tall one guffawed the while the other
was sayin' "Good mornin', grey sweet mother!"

EMIGRANT

I think of her,
the quiet and the peace,
the yellow of the furze,
the rivers, without ceasing;

the somber moods
of the mountains and the cliffs,
the fairy woodlands,
the boats gently lifting!

The narrow walk
with a spire at the end,
my brothers talking
with old, old friends,

I think of her
and stir my tea.
God! I wonder,
Do ever they speak of me?

VI. AROUND IRELAND

LYRICS TO ACCOMPANY A LUTE

The hill doesn't seem
so high today
and the wind is pushin'
my cycle along,
and the gulls are burstin'
out in song,
For I'm marryin' Danny O'Shea!

A thousand times
I've seen the bay
from the top o' the hill,
oh, blue of blues,
today it's shimmerin'
with the news
That I'm marryin' Danny O'Shea!

A cottage we'll build us
by the bay,
and there we'll be makin'
the grand decision
to buy a cow
or television,
Me and my Danny O'Shea!

JUST LISTENING

The rain's dissected drop by drop,
today is *soft* or *shocking,*
the cabbage and potato crop
turn on a tide of talking,

on village corners, clear as chimes
are world affairs berated,
from doorways drift the Troubled Times
recapitulated,

the tankard's lifted in the pub
and eloquently clinked,
the Dáil's debating on a sub-
ject meant to be succinct:

the men of Ireland have no peers,
no matter what their station,
from castled earls to garreteers,
the password's *conversation,*

for talk they do and talk they must;
to visitors it's very
evident that life is just
a running commentary

and Irishmen on Judgment Day,
en route to sweet salvation,
will catch their breath in such a way
as exhales conversation.

A BROTH OF A GIRL

Her name can be Mary Kathleen Mullins
with curls as flaming as Cuchulain's,

or raven-haired as a Spanish mate
shipwrecked in fifteen eighty-eight,

she may be a colleen at first guess;
she's not *a broth of a girl* unless

there's plenty o' meat on her healthy bones
with legs that are worth their weight in stones:

> not tall and lean,
> not thin and lanky
> nor wispy as
> a linen hanky;

her eyes may be green as County Kerry,
her cheeks as red as a holly berry,

brow as milky as mother-of-pearl
but lads, she's not *a broth of a girl*

> unless your arms
> must stretch a bit
> around her waist
> to make them fit,

and who'd be wanting a froth of a girl
when there's more to love in *a broth of a girl?*

TOURIST SEASON

AMERICA

Dear Sir,
 I'm planning a vacation:
 Are you handy to the beaches
 With drugstore and a movie very near?

 If you have an elevator,
 Can assure me steaming water,
 Please reserve a room for me, two weeks, third floor.

IRELAND

Dear Madam,
 You'll enjoy your holiday:
 We are rather close to strands,
 With chemist and the pictures sort of near.

 Our lift moves quite efficiently,
 Our geyser warms sufficiently,
 We'll book you for a fortnight, second storey.

LINES WRITTEN UNDER A PALM TREE
IN PARKNASILLA

It's said when Christopher Columbus
paused in Ireland that he stayed
in Galway, and St. Nicholas' Church
is where he knelt and prayed.

And while he prayed his little ships
would safely ply the ocean's rim,
a swarthy Irish sea-lad begged
to risk the unknown depths with him.

History failed to jot his name,
some disbelieve the legend, but
someone sailed back from tropic isles,
someone brought a coconut.

AT BALLYNAHINCH

In a moment of economy
God wrought the moor and bluff
of Mayo . . . then suddenly
He must have thought *Enough!*

At Ballynahinch tall trees arise
as if a line were drawn
abruptly as a green surprise
for man to come upon.

Summoning water, icy-clear,
God lingered for a minute:
Such beauty calls for challenge here,
and slid pink salmon in it.

ON FALLING OVER A CANNON
AT POWERSCOURT

Once you boomed beneath the trees,
Bringing a village to its knees;
Then impotent and antiquated,
For rusty centuries you waited
For revenge on your lost power. . . .

Whom the victim . . . when the hour?
In the Great Hall, crouching black,
Without a charge, without a noise,
You tripped my leg and pulled me back
To sudden tears and shattered poise.

NOON AT WEXFORD HARBOUR

The world unfurled . . . half sky, half sea;
one half was lapis lazuli
that leisurely smoothed from the bay
and disappeared, horizon-grey,

from whence the sky commenced and curved
uncommonly till, cirrus-blurred,
noon became an azure arch
starred by a single bird.

COASTAL WIVES

Winter keeps the coastal wives together
When morning's late and spray is bitter cold;
Flung in and out of doors they watch the weather
and talk in whispers as the day unfolds,
With silences of whipping waves and yawls
And fear wrapped 'round them smothering as shawls.

Summertime shakes out the wives from houses
as wives would shake a blanket out to air;
The smell of June is on the sunny grasses
And handkerchiefs are fluttering everywhere.
No man on such a day could come to harm
With sky so open and the sea so warm.

SOLITUDE IN ENNISKILLEN

After the November storm
Will ever the woods be dry again?
Will ever the sun appear to warm
And loosen life along this lane
Depressed with rain?

The air is dim with lassitude:
Presuméd now, the squirrel and mouse;
Rabbit, hunched in sodden mood,
Red fox, prone beneath limp boughs
Where jewel-flies drowse.

The scumbled path of twig and root
Is puddle-bright. A week ago
Brown burrs and berries underfoot
Remarked as stoats would come and go.
Today it is not so.

Cathedral-tall, the ancient trees
Sag silver-green with gossamer.
Nothing moves except for me,
No leaf descends, no pigeon whirrs,
No wet fern stirs.

IN A DRAWING ROOM IN KILLAVULLEN
(1846)

"Jessica, why are you sitting very still,
twirling your hair around your finger so?
Your doll lies broken by the garden grille,
your face is white as snow."

*"Because I had a terrible nightmare
and I was frightened, Nanny, and today
the dream is with me everywhere
and will not go away."*

"And now, what dream could cloud your pretty head,
a little girl as sheltered as a princess?
I was sleeping safely near your bed.
Don't twist your poplin dress!"

*"I dreamed that County Cork was burned and black,
black even in the daytime, and I cried
because along the road the bones were stacked
of people who had died."*

"Jessica! July is getting late
and you sit crumpled in your pinafore.
Promise me you won't go near the gate,
but run and play outdoors."

*"Oh, Nanny, I went to the gate this morning
and it was even worse than yesterday.
I hid and saw poor people standing moaning
and heard the things they say."*

"Please love, it's only crops; you mustn't worry,
we'll be on holiday across the sea
this time next week. Jessica, now hurry
and tidy up for tea!"

EIVLIN, EIVLIN
(Bunratty Castle, Fifteenth Century)

Love is more than prophets have said. . . .
Love is round as the slow moon going,
Soft, oh, soft as the down of a lover's bed,
Warm as the woolen cape when night is blowing.

> *Eivlin, Eivlin, love is pale,*
> *Love is sickly, love is frail.*

Love is lingering as the muted lyre,
Love is cloistered as the hand-cupped candle,
Is silken as the plait of waist-long hair,
As woven as the small brocaded sandal.

> *Eivlin, Eivlin, love is harsh*
> *As the quicksand in the marsh.*

Love is secret as the lowered bridge,
Love is silent as the mossy water,
Is pure-white as the steed behind the hedge,
As heathered as the wind at the midnight hour.

> *Eivlin, Eivlin, now or never,*
> *Flee the bleak and ruined tower.*

APPROACH TO ENNISKERRY

Granite flexing at the turn,
Grass tilting from the fence
Into this hollow of a town
Of greenest consequence,

A traveller centuries from now
Will glean beyond the bend
Blue sea, a dickey in the hills,
And treetops that descend

Toward pricking spire and peat smoke
And gentleness of word,
And quickly down this Wicklow slope
He'll stumble, reassured.

THE GHOST OF LEIXLIP CASTLE
(County Kildare)

I am the ghost of Leixlip Castle
rustling down the winding stair;
nay, 'tis not a murdered vassal
vengeful in the windy tower
who wanders at the midnight hour,
forsooth, 'tis I, 'tis I!

The villagers believe at night
a venturesome twelfth-century nun,
starved for salmon, drifts in white,
her habit streaming cold moonlight
down where the waters run,
alas, it is not so!

The burning ears of spectral hounds
appear at thousands of *carreaux*
tonight to catch the swishing sounds
of taffeta, as soft I go
toward the new master's candle-glow;
suddenly he stirs!

Stepping lightly on the weathered
boards that murmur while he sleeps
I dryly mince and trail my feathered
ocelli in silken sweeps;
he wakes, as close a peacock creeps,
the ghost of Leixlip Castle!

"Castels repaired at the comon chardge

M^d that yn the yere of our Lorde Gode MCCCCC°
and in the xvj^{en} yere of the rayne of kynge Henry vij^{th}
John Archer beyng souerayne of Kilkenny
the Castell gate Saynt Patrickes gate
Saynt James ys gate and the Walkynge gate
was nywe made and repaired at the comon coste
whiche cost vij lib. xiijs. *id* ob.
excepte the bordes vj peces tymbre mete and drinke."

From: *Liber Primus Kilkenniensis,* 1500

LETTER OF PROTEST

John Archer, sir, I see the billing's
seven pounds and thirteen shillings
for making new the Castle gates;
and I submit such shocking rates
for labor-cost extremely large,
albeit it is the common charge.

Granted, we should not be lax
in fortifying 'gainst attacks;
but it's outrageous, I aver:
one pound and eighteen shillings, sir,
to mend each gate and make it new.
What *is* Kilkenny coming to?

THE HOLY SEED

Cromlechs crumble by the sea,
Ruined shells lie scarred and scattered—
A dolmen prone upon a lea,
A monastery strewn and shattered
By the war-cry of the Norse,
A lonely crozier lapped in gorse.

Now a relic draped in moss,
The tower reflected in the river;
Massive mounds of ivy gloss
A chapel arch with verdant cover
Where echoes of the pagan Vikings
Startled kneeling monks and High Kings.

Sunk beneath these ancient walls
The grains of Christianity
Spread their roots through Eire's hills,
Flowering for humanity.
And from grey pods, the priests, like birds,
Carry the seed of the Holy Words.

COUNTY MAYO

Centuries, for cotters,
is the slow unwinding
of stone walls molded
over barren sod.

Time is sons and daughters,
wind and water binding
generations welded
by stone and God.

THE ORPHANS' BAND
IN TRALEE

Quiet followed bright fanfare
at the Kingdom County Fair . . .

except for muted mooing sounds
all was silence on the grounds

as the leader of the Band
cut a flourish with his hand:

softly fumbling for the key,
St. Joseph's Boys' Band of Tralee

let fly the notes that they had learned
recently; each tone was earned

by blowing hard on flute and horn
until a melody was borne,

rippling as the flag, and loud,
above the solemn Kerry crowd.

Francis Scott Key would have stood
with thumping heart and called it good

if he had heard Star-Spangled Banner
played in such a reverent manner.

SUMMER PRISM

I can't let go
of certain days—
Adare,
so effortlessly mine,
dropped me
precisely into place
in a rare
kaleidoscope design
of Desmond Castle,
postcard-still,
and twilight creeping
on the hill.

The village roofs
are thatched with gold
and men are drifting
to their doors.
Ireland!
Let me pause
and hold
this day to me
before it soars
moonward
from this Limerick glen,
and chill comes up
and drives me in.

MEMORIAL

Loved ones, light the torches
Beside this earthly quarter
That in his name eternal flame
Bear witness to the martyr

The while the Irish pipes lament
The Mist over the Mountain.

Arlington Cemetery
November 25, 1963